GROUP
→ *Video Experience* ←

TONY EVANS
CHRYSTAL EVANS HURST

KINGDOM
WOMAN

EMBRACING YOUR PURPOSE,
POWER, AND POSSIBILITIES

D0967225

TYNDALE HOUSE PUBLISHERS, INC.
CAROL STREAM, ILLINOIS

Kingdom Woman Group Video Experience
Study Guide

Copyright © 2014 Focus on the Family

ISBN: 978-1-62405-210-1

Based on the book *Kingdom Woman* by Dr. Tony Evans and Chrystal Evans Hurst, © 2013 Tony Evans and Chrystal Evans Hurst. Published by Tyndale House Publishers, Inc., and Focus on the Family.

Focus on the Family and the accompanying logo and design are federally registered trademarks of Focus on the Family, 8605 Explorer Drive, Colorado Springs, CO 80920.

A Focus on the Family book published by Tyndale House Publishers, Carol Stream, Illinois 60188

TYNDALE is a registered trademark of Tyndale House Publishers, Inc. Tyndale's quill logo is a trademark of Tyndale House Publishers, Inc.

All Scripture quotations, unless otherwise indicated, are taken from the *New American Standard Bible*®. Copyright © 1960, 1962, 1963, 1968, 1971, 1972, 1973, 1975, 1977, 1995 by The Lockman Foundation. Used by permission. (www.Lockman.org).

Scripture quotations marked (ESV) are from *The Holy Bible, English Standard Version*®, (ESV®). Copyright © 2001 by Crossway, a publishing ministry of Good News Publishers. Used by permission. All rights reserved.

Scripture quotations marked (KJV) are taken from the *Holy Bible, King James Version*.

All italicized words in Scripture quotations were added by the author for emphasis.

No part of this publication may be reproduced, stored in a retrieval system, or transmitted in any form or by any means—electronic, mechanical, photocopy, recording, or otherwise—without prior permission of Focus on the Family.

Cover design by Jennifer Ghionzoli
Cover skyline photo copyright © PhotoDisc. All rights reserved.
Cover photograph taken by Stephen Vosloo. © Focus on the Family.

Printed in the United States of America
2 3 4 5 6 7 / 20 19 18 17 16 15 14

CONTENTS

WELCOME, KINGDOM WOMAN!

Walking in the way of a kingdom woman is transformational. Beginning now, you can discover your true spiritual destiny by experiencing this dynamic DVD course. It's straightforward, easy-to-use, and most important—fun.

At the core of each session is a video presentation featuring one of the authors of *Kingdom Woman*: Dr. Tony Evans or his daughter Chrystal Evans Hurst. Plus, this package includes a special appearance by Tony Evans's wife, Lois Evans. The Evans family offers inspired teaching that will give you new insights into biblical principles as well as assurance that God tenderly loves each and every kingdom woman.

In each chapter of this book, you'll find the following sections:

The Gathering
Read this brief excerpt to focus on the subject at hand.

Show Time!
Use this section as you view and think about the DVD presentation; it includes thought-provoking questions and biblical input.

So What?
This section helps you apply what you've learned to your life.

Transformation Moments
This brief wrap-up will help you find encouragement and presents a challenge to try this week.

Note: The video presentations and this guide are intended as general advice only and not meant to replace clinical counseling, medical treatment, legal counsel, or pastoral guidance.

Focus on the Family maintains a referral network of Christian counselors. For information, call 1-800-A-FAMILY and ask for the counseling department. You can also find plenty of parenting advice and encouragement at www.focusonthefamily.com.

1

❧

THE VALUE OF A
KINGDOM WOMAN

The Main Point

Regardless of what the culture says, kingdom women are valuable
to God.

The Gathering

Getting Your Thoughts Together

To find out more about what a kingdom woman is, read the following book excerpt and answer the questions that appear at the end.

A KINGDOM WOMAN'S STILETTOS

by Chrystal Evans Hurst

Kingdom woman. Those words sound like some pretty high stilettos to walk
around in all day. The truth of the matter is that I know I'm not that woman.
She is someone I strive to become but whose roles and responsibilities seem
like a lot to handle. The very definition of a kingdom woman sets a high

bar. After all, where is this woman—who is this woman—who regularly and consistently positions herself under and operates according to God's complete rule over her life? . . .

I desire to be the woman that He created me to be—not the woman whom I think I want to be or the woman the world tells me I should be. It brings me great joy to think of the detailed design and intricate effort that God put forth when making me. I'm so glad that I don't have to aspire to be anyone else other than that woman God wants me to be.

You don't have to seek anyone else's approval for the life God has given you to live. You don't have to apologize for the strength, fortitude, courage, talent, beauty, or intellect your Creator has given you. Ladies, we all are "God's workmanship, created in Christ Jesus to do good works, which God prepared in advance for us to do" (Ephesians 2:10).

Kingdom woman. Those four-inch red heels don't look easy to walk around in all day. But first looks can be deceiving. The right shoe made by the right designer and with the right materials can be not just wearable but comfortable! God has designed a plan and a purpose for you. You are not just "fearfully and wonderfully made" (Psalm 139:14); you are created in the image of a radiant, magnificent God who is full of beauty and splendor. So wear His glory well. Walk on His runway.[1]

Why is it easy to believe that other women are the true kingdom women and not ourselves? Why do kingdom women look at all of the things they aren't—thin, rich, witty, fluent in six biblical languages—instead of looking at themselves as being created in the image of God?

Show Time!

Viewing and Examining the DVD Content

In this portion of the DVD, Tony Evans turns mannequins into metaphors for Christian living. Mannequins, he says, represent the store, or kingdom, of their owners. They are displayed to lure people off the street and into the department store kingdom. As kingdom women, they are on display for God. They are to model kingdom life and "lure" people into the kingdom of God.

∞

After viewing the presentation "The Value of a Kingdom Woman," use the following questions to help you think through what you saw and heard.

1. Dr. Evans compares kingdom women to mannequins when he says, "The [department store] owners put them on display in order to attract us off the street into a kingdom called Saks. Unless people come off the street and into the store, they won't get the benefit of all that the kingdom has to offer. . . . Ladies, God has placed you on display, and He wants you to be a showstopper for another King and another kingdom."

   If someone were to turn you into a department store fashion mannequin right now, which department store would you like to represent?
   • Macy's
   • David's Bridal
   • Dillard's
   • Lands' End
   • DICK'S Sporting Goods
   • Abercrombie and Fitch
   • Goodwill
   • other _____

   How many people would be attracted to your fashion style enough to go inside the store?

Today, if your spiritual gifts were on display for God, which department in the heavenly kingdom would you best represent? (1 Corinthians 12: 4–11.)

- wisdom
- faith
- miracles
- knowledge
- healing
- discernment
- prophecy
- other _____

Is it easier to understand your place in the kingdom of fashion or in the spiritual kingdom?

2. Dr. Evans defines a kingdom woman as "a female who consistently positions herself, places herself, and operates under the rule of God in her life." Is that different from the way you've been defining your walk with God? If so, how? What do you think about Tony's definition?

3. Let's look at Tony Evans's main text for this session, Genesis 1:26–27.

> Then God said, "Let us make man in our image, in our
> likeness, and let them rule over the fish of the sea and the
> birds of the air, over the livestock, over all the earth, and over
> all the creatures that move along the ground." So God
> created man in his own image, in the image of God he
> created him; male and female he created them.

Are women created in the image of God in the same way that men are created in His image? Is there anything in this passage that implies women are somehow created in an inferior way to men? What does it mean to be "created in the image of God"?

4. Is the concept that God fashioned Eve from Adam's rib—that she is an *ezer kenegdo*[2] helper and not a subordinate (translate: secretary, assistant, second-class citizen, cook, cleaner, child raiser, dish washer)—a new concept to you? What have you

previously been taught about a woman's role in marriage or the church? Tony Evans states in the presentation, "There is no difference in equality of being, value, or dignity between the genders." Is that a liberating thought for you? In what ways?

5. Tony Evans asserts that undisciplined men are "dissin'" God when they treat women as less than essential and equal partners. God holds women in such high regard that He will not even listen to a man's prayers when he does not honor his wife as an equal heir in God's kingdom. First Peter 3:7 says, "Husbands, in the same way be considerate as you live with your wives, and treat them with respect, . . . as heirs with you of the gracious gift of life so that nothing will hinder your prayers." God champions women to the extent that He will withhold blessings from the husband who disrespects his wife. Have you ever seen this principle at work? How does having God as a champion make you feel?

6. What was your reaction when Tony Evans spat on the one-hundred-dollar bill?
   - Bring out the disinfectant!
   - Isn't it illegal to deface legal tender?
   - Ben Franklin just rolled in his grave.
   - I thought Tony's mom (or Lois!) had taught him better manners!
   - other _____

   What was Tony trying to convey with that object lesson?

7. Read the following excerpt, and reflect on the questions at the end.

GOD IS EVERY KINGDOM WOMAN'S FIRST HUSBAND

by Tony Evans

Eve's first calling was to God—to fulfill His purpose for her life, which in her case was to help Adam. Her role as helpmate was not just a role of companionship; it also included a significant role as collaborator in the dominion mandate.

Yet many women today—either because of divorce or a lack of kingdom men to even marry—do not have an Adam to help. If you are one of these women, take courage and pride in your calling, because God alone is your purpose. You have been made for Him. As He said in Isaiah,

> "For your Maker is your husband—the Lord Almighty is his name—the Holy One of Israel is your Redeemer; he is called the God of all the earth. The Lord will call you back as if you were a wife deserted and distressed in spirit—a wife who married young, only to be rejected," says your God. (54:5–6)

Whether you are married on earth or if God is your Husband (Isaiah 54:5), your worth is far above any treasure. One of the most important truths you need to believe concerns your worth. You are significant. You are valuable. You are worth more than jewels. As a kingdom woman who fears the Lord, guard your value by first making sure you view yourself according to the value God has given to you. You are to do all you can to ensure that others treat you with dignity. You are to be treated as a treasure, not as someone to be trashed or used.

I understand that there are situations where you may not be able to control how you are treated, but that doesn't mean you have to acquiesce to it. You do not have to internally accept someone else's denigration of you. It should not affect your view of who you are. As Eleanor Roosevelt said, "No one can make you feel inferior without your consent."[3]

You are first and foremost a kingdom woman created for God's work. Your life, through His sustaining strength, ought to be one of great purpose, spiritual power, and possibilities.[4]

Based on this excerpt, what would you say is the primary purpose of a kingdom woman?

So What?
Helping It All Make Sense

Kingdom Woman Meets *Antiques Roadshow*

In the DVD session, Tony Evans tells the story of a woman who was selling a table for six hundred dollars. After recounting its value, she raised the price to one thousand dollars.

Now let's imagine that you're on the PBS program *Antiques Roadshow*. You've been waiting at a crowded convention center for two days for your turn to meet an official *Antiques Roadshow* appraiser. Suddenly your name is called. You flush with excitement and step up on a dais covered in plush green carpet. The other people waiting turn toward you, gaping in anticipation. An intelligent-looking, impeccably dressed gentlemen begins to inspect you. You fear he may actually check your teeth!

First, he asks the usual questions: "How old are you?" "Where did you originate?" "Why are you here today?"

Like a fashion model, you pivot and turn so he can examine your person from all angles.

Then comes the speech where the appraiser lists your flaws: (Fill in what you believe to be your greatest shortcomings. List the mean things people have said to you over the years. List people in your life who may be disappointed in you because you haven't lived up to their expectations: your parents, your children, your coworkers, your friends, your teachers, or even your husband. In general terms, list the sins you've committed and the bad habits that you think stain your character.)

Now comes the interesting part of the show (the part that keeps this sleeper of a program on the air). It's finally time for the appraiser, after listing all your defects, to declare your true value.

He says, "Yes, there are certainly flaws, and one would expect that of someone derived from Adam and Eve's lineage, but . . . in this owners manual"—he pulls a small Bible out of his pocket—"it verifies you were created in God's image . . . " He begins to read from several passages and then declares, "Your worth is far beyond rubies. You are a priceless treasure. You are a daughter of God!"

The audience erupts into enthusiastic applause.

(Take out your Bible and read the verses in their entirety or use the key phrases listed beside the Scripture reference. Fill in the reasons below that you have worth and value in God's eyes.)

- Psalm 8:5—"crowned [you] with glory and honor"
- Psalm 139:13–16—"fearfully and wonderfully made"
- Proverbs 31:10—"She is worth far more than rubies"
- Isaiah 1:18—"Though your sins are like scarlet, they shall be as white as snow"
- Isaiah 58:10–11—"The Lord will guide you always"
- Jeremiah 29:11—"plans to prosper you . . . to give you a hope and a future"
- Jeremiah 31:3—"I have loved you with an everlasting love; I have drawn you with unfailing kindness"
- Zephaniah 3:17—"[God] will rejoice over you with singing"
- Luke 7:47—"her many sins have been forgiven"
- Luke 12:6–7—"You are worth more than many sparrows"
- John 3:16–17—"For God so loved the world . . . whoever believes in [Jesus] . . . will have eternal life"
- Romans 5:8—"Christ died for us"
- Romans 8:37–39—"[nothing] will be able to separate us from the love of God"
- 1 John 3:1—"See what great love the Father has lavished on us"
- 1 John 3:16—"Jesus Christ laid down his life for us"

How did this exercise help you confirm your value in God's eyes? How did reflecting on the Bible verses influence the way you think about yourself as a kingdom woman?

Transformation Moments
Taking the Next Step at Home
Read the following Bible passage (Proverbs 31:10–31, esv) and excerpt, and then reflect on the questions at the end.

"The Proverbs 31 Woman"
An excellent wife who can find?
She is far more precious than jewels.
The heart of her husband trusts in her,
    and he will have no lack of gain.
She does him good, and not harm,
    all the days of her life.
She seeks wool and flax,

and works with willing hands.
She is like the ships of the merchant;
   she brings her food from afar.
She rises while it is yet night
   and provides food for her household
   and portions for her maidens.
She considers a field and buys it;
   with the fruit of her hands she plants a vineyard.
She dresses herself with strength
   and makes her arms strong.
She perceives that her merchandise is profitable.
Her lamp does not go out at night.
She puts her hands to the distaff,
   and her hands hold the spindle.
She opens her hand to the poor
   and reaches out her hands to the needy.
She is not afraid of snow for her household,
   for all her household are clothed in scarlet.
She makes bed coverings for herself;
   her clothing is fine linen and purple.
Her husband is known in the gates
   when he sits among the elders of the land.

She makes linen garments and sells them;
    she delivers sashes to the merchant.
Strength and dignity are her clothing,
    and she laughs at the time to come.
She opens her mouth with wisdom,
    and the teaching of kindness is on her tongue.
She looks well to the ways of her household
    and does not eat the bread of idleness.
Her children rise up and call her blessed;
    her husband also, and he praises her:
"Many women have done excellently,
    but you surpass them all."
Charm is deceitful, and beauty is vain,
    but a woman who fears the Lord is to be praised.
Give her of the fruit of her hands,
    and let her works praise her in the gates.

The wife described is a kingdom woman fully engaged, and her worth is "far more than rubies." Single women can also follow her example in principle, especially in the community sphere.

Read the following *Kingdom Woman* book excerpt titled "The Proverbs 31 Kingdom Woman."

THE PROVERBS 31 KINGDOM WOMAN
by Tony Evans

The Proverbs 31 woman is the hallmark of kingdom women. I like to call her a woman for all seasons. She is strong, intelligent, capable, giving, resourceful, efficient, spiritually minded, and much more.

I know that sounds like she is a perfect woman, and you may feel that her standard is set too high to actually reach. But the Proverbs 31 woman is not the model of a perfect woman. Neither is a kingdom woman called to perfection. Let's use a stay-at-home mom as just one example. A kingdom woman is not someone who can multitask perfectly while also homeschooling three very different children, serving on four church committees, carpooling eleven neighborhood kids back and forth to soccer, keeping her home spotless, coaching the spelling-bee team . . . making her husband have the best night of his life each and every evening, and maintaining a size 6 figure well into her fifties—all while cooking only organic, nongenetically modified foods and making every meal from scratch.

That woman doesn't exist. And we didn't put this book together to make you think that you should be her either. In fact, from my experience pastoring a church for nearly four decades and spending thousands of hours counseling both women and men, the issue is often that women are trying to do too much—and all at once.

Women, you can be a Proverbs 31 woman and more—but that doesn't mean you do it all at the same time. One of the most important principles for you as a kingdom woman is that your life flows through different seasons. Each of these seasons carries with it different time constraints, blessings, and demands. To try to do all things without being cognizant of the season you are in is the surest way to burnout and even bitterness. The primary foundation of being a kingdom woman doesn't include a million different things done a million different ways. The primary foundation is actually simple and straightforward. It is located at the end of Proverbs 31. After listing everything that this particular woman did, the verse says,

> Charm is deceptive, and beauty is fleeting;
>> but a woman who fears the Lord is to be praised.
> Give her the reward she has earned,
>> and let her works bring her praise at the city gate. (Verses 30–31)

What sets a kingdom woman apart from any other women boils down to her fear of God. Her reverence determines her actions, thoughts, words, and priorities. Without that, the demands of life would overwhelm any woman.[5]

A kingdom woman's value is intrinsic; however, her ability to serve God well is dependent upon her willingness to "fear" Him and allow Him to prioritize her tasks.

2

THE MAKING OF A KINGDOM WOMAN

The Main Point

We are all flawed and dirty with sin, but Jesus goes out of His way to find us anyway.

The Gathering

Getting Your Thoughts Together

To find out more about the way Jesus searches for us, read the following book excerpt and answer the questions that appear at the end.

THE SAMARITAN OUTCAST

by Chrystal Evans Hurst

The Samaritan woman was startled when Jesus spoke directly to her. And she should have been. In that day and age, Jews did not associate with Samaritans. They were the underclass, the despised, the second-rate citizens. In John 4:9, she said, "You are a Jew and I am a Samaritan woman. How can you ask me for a drink?"

Samaritans were not considered to be of "pure" ancestry. They were not considered true descendants of the Jewish patriarchs. They were believed to be a race of people who resulted from intermarriage between Hebrews and Assyrians after Assyria invaded and conquered the northern kingdom of Israel around 721 BC. They were a group of people who were considered defiled both racially and spiritually. They were thought to be unworthy, unimportant, and unvalued by those who considered themselves "true Jews" or people with a right to a sacred heritage.

The woman at the well actually had two strikes against her: She was a Samaritan, and, well, she was a woman! It was not accepted practice for a Jewish man to speak with a woman in public. Further, it is suspected that she was not well respected as a woman in her own community either.

The Samaritan woman went to draw water from the well at noon (John 4:6). This would have been the hottest part of the day, so it is implied that she went at this time to avoid going at the same time as most of the other women who would draw water from the well. She did not want to mix with people who might look down on her or ridicule her. This woman did not meet the standard for Jews. This woman didn't even meet the standards of her own community. She was an outcast.

And Jesus talked to her.[1]

What social customs was Jesus breaking when he talked to this woman? Why was she there alone? Was she expecting a Jewish man dressed in rabbi's garb to speak to her? Why or why not?

Show Time!

Viewing and Examining the DVD Content

In this portion of the DVD, Chrystal Evans Hurst begins the story about the Samaritan woman at the well from John 4. She uses diamond mining as a metaphor for the way Jesus "mines" for us. All of us, she says, are dirty, buried deep in the ground of sin, before Jesus finds us and begins the refining process.

∽

After viewing the presentation "The Making of a Kingdom Woman," use the following questions to help you think through what you saw and heard.

1. The Koh-I-Noor and Sancy Diamonds are declared "priceless," while the Hope and Cullinan Diamonds are valued at a bargain—less than five-hundred-million dollars a piece.[2] All

diamonds have what's called an inclusion, or flaw. Even the "perfect" ones have a bubble, crack, ripple, or discoloration that can be seen when they are examined under extreme magnification.[3] Despite their flaws, diamonds are one of the most valued gems on earth.

In what way is Jesus like a diamond miner? In what ways is a kingdom woman like a diamond in the earth?

2. Chrystal quotes Ezekiel 34:16—"I will search for the lost" and John 15:16—"You did not choose me, but I chose you." Sometimes, however, kingdom women don't feel as if they deserve to be chosen by Jesus. They realize that they are "dirty" and encased in kimberlite. They know they are not ready to be displayed. Verses such as Romans 3:23 describe this reality spot-on: "For all have sinned and fall short of the glory of God."

Why might it be a good thing for a kingdom woman to remember that she "came from the dirt"?

3. Chrystal informs us about the history of Jacob's Well and what the city near it (called Sychar or Shechem) represented: disobedience followed by blessing. It was no accident that Jesus spoke to the Samaritan woman in this symbolic and historic place. Chrystal says it was as if Jesus were saying, "What I've done for one, I can do for you."

   Why should kingdom women share their testimonies with others? What is the purpose of telling other people about the good things God has done in their lives?

4. If the Samaritan woman wrote a book, it might be titled *Kimberlite Woman*. She certainly wasn't ready for display—and she knew it. That's why she came to the well at the hottest part of the day when no one else should have been there. She didn't have the right DNA. She didn't have the right religion. She didn't have the right lifestyle. She probably didn't even have the right clothes.

   But Jesus spoke to her, asking, "Will you give me a drink?" Why did he speak to her?

Do you believe Jesus gives you the same opportunity for time and attention as He gave to the Samaritan woman? Why or why not?

5. Read the following excerpt, and reflect on the questions at the end.

FLAWED

by Chrystal Evans Hurst

A kingdom woman is not a perfect woman. She is a forgiven woman. She is a woman who has been loved by the Master despite her past, her weaknesses, or her struggles. She is bold. She is the woman who, because she has nothing left to lose, puts it all on the line to point others to the Giver of Life.

The kingdom woman does not limit herself to lines drawn by our society across racial, socioeconomic, or cultural lines.

She is a woman who recognizes her own depravity, either because she has been on the edge of a pit, fallen into a pit, or wallowed in the mud. She is amazed that Jesus has gone out of His way to know her by name. And because she is astonished that Jesus did not think her too low or unworthy of salvation, she is grateful.[4]

Based on this excerpt, what personal comfort can you find from the story about the Samaritan woman?

So What?

Helping It All Make Sense

Take a few minutes to read through the "Kimberlite Woman Self-Test" and answer the questions that follow it.

Kimberlite Woman Self-Test

In DVD session 2, Chrystal Evans Hurst tells the story of a friend who was looking for a diamond engagement ring. She was selecting from the diamonds ready for display. But before a diamond is ever set out in the marketplace, it must first be mined, which is an expensive process. One important step in that process is selecting the best place to look for diamonds. However, even in a known gem-rich region, mines can be opened that yield poorly. And not all diamonds are found in the same way. In very rare instances is a diamond discovered with relatively little effort. That was the case of the Cullinan Diamond, also called the Star of Africa. In 1905, a mine inspector saw a glint in the wall of a mineshaft. He reached over with his pocketknife and pried out the crystal chunk. That rock was a diamond twice the size of any previously discovered.[5]

Now take this short self-test to help you reflect on the spiritual mining process you've experienced.

Indicate your answer by marking a spot on the line between one thought and the other.

1. When God found me, I was . . .

_____

embedded deep in the earth's crust   buried just beneath
                                                  the surface

2. When God found me, I was . . .

_____

covered in kimberlite   showing a lot of potential crystal

3. When God found me, I knew . . .

_____

a lot of finished "diamonds"   didn't know any gem-quality
                                                  people

4. When God found me, I erroneously thought . . .

_____

I was a polished gem already   I was only a chunk of asphalt

5. When God found me, I felt . . .

glad and a little frightened	angry because I didn't want to leave my core

6. When God found me, I believed . . .

there was no real "Miner"	there was a "Miner" who knew every gem

7. Now that I have been found, I feel . . .

like a sparkly diamond chip	like a 100-carat masterpiece

8. Now that I have been found, I want . . .

to enjoy the polishing process	to hurry up and be put on display

How did this exercise help you understand the "mining" process of becoming a daughter of God? Did you do anything to get yourself out of the kimberlite? Who did all the work?

How does Ephesians 2:8–9 apply to the finding process? "For it is by grace you have been saved, through faith—and this not from yourselves, it is the gift of God—not by works, so that no one can boast."

Transformation Moments

Taking the Next Step at Home

Read the following Bible passage (1 Kings 17:7–16, ESV) and excerpt, and then reflect on the questions at the end.

"THE WIDOW OF ZAREPHATH"

Some time later the brook dried up because there had been no rain in the land. Then the word of the LORD came to him: "Go at once to Zarephath in the region of Sidon and stay there. I have directed a widow there to supply you with food." So he went to Zarephath. When he came to the town gate, a widow was there gathering sticks. He called to her and asked, "Would you bring me a little water in a jar so I may have a drink?" As she was going to get it, he called, "And bring me, please, a piece of bread."

"As surely as the LORD your God lives," she replied, "I don't have any bread—only a handful of flour in a jar and a little olive oil in a jug. I am gathering a few sticks to take home and make a meal for myself and my son, that we may eat it—and die."

Elijah said to her, "Don't be afraid. Go home and do as you have said. But first make a small loaf of bread for me from what you have and bring it to me, and then make something for yourself and your son. For this is what the LORD, the God of

Israel, says: 'The jar of flour will not be used up and the jug of oil will not run dry until the day the LORD sends rain on the land.'"

She went away and did as Elijah had told her. So there was food every day for Elijah and for the woman and her family. For the jar of flour was not used up and the jug of oil did not run dry, in keeping with the word of the LORD spoken by Elijah.

Read the following book excerpt and reflect on the question that follows it.

THE WIDOW OF ZAREPHATH
by Tony Evans

In 1 Kings, we come across another "outsider" woman whom God chose to set apart for a good work. A famine had hit the land where she lived, making it difficult for her to survive. The economy had crumbled, and the country was experiencing far more than a recession. It was a depression affecting countless individuals.

God had instructed the prophet Elijah to go to a place called Zarephath, where a widow lived. God told Elijah that He had commanded the widow to provide for Elijah. Elijah knew that she was down to her last serving of grain. But Elijah told her that if she would make him a cake, then she could make some for herself and her son as well. God had said there would be enough for all of them.

It didn't make sense. In fact, it was downright ridiculous. Yet God had asked.

And she obeyed in faith.

This is my take on the passage: God hadn't chosen her randomly. Her actions, thoughts, and decisions leading up to that point had made her a woman who caught God's special attention.

Besides that, she lived outside of Israel in the Phoenician city of Sidon. God didn't go to the "church" to find the woman He was going to use. He didn't go down and visit the nearest Bible study. This is because sometimes the greatest faith is found in the most surprising places, simply because faith depends upon relationship rather than religion.

When God looked for someone to ultimately save the ministry of His prophet Elijah at a time of great trial and need, He didn't even go to a man. There certainly were many men at that time with access to some food. Yet at this crucial moment in Elijah's calling as a prophet, God intentionally singled out a kingdom woman to save the day.[6]

Like the Samaritan woman, the widow of Zarephath was on the margins of society. She had no one to help her raise her son, and she was out of food and had been starving for a long time. There is no mention of an extended family helping her. She was also outside the region where most Jews lived. She was ready to give up and die! And then God chose her and sent a special servant to show His care.

Which woman do you relate to more: the widow or the woman at the well?

3

THE REFINING OF A KINGDOM WOMAN

The Main Point

After God finds a kingdom woman, He will refine her.

The Gathering

Getting Your Thoughts Together

To find out more about the spiritual refining process, read the following book excerpt and answer the questions that appear at the end.

WATER THAT CAN CHANGE LIVES

by Chrystal Evans Hurst

In John 4, Jesus asked the Samaritan woman at the well to give Him some water. He invited her into an interaction, a conversation, a discussion about a gift that was available—even for her.

Then He offered her living water. Water that would satisfy. Water that came from the Man who knew about her stained life and wanted to give her a gift from God anyway.

And the Samaritan woman wanted the gift. "Sir, give me this water so that I won't get thirsty and have to keep coming here to draw water" (verse 15). She wanted this living water so badly that she was willing to let Jesus call her out on her lifestyle (verses 16–19). She desired this living water so much that she sought to understand the difference between religion and a personal relationship with Christ (verses 20–26). This woman needed living water so desperately that with eager abandon, she left her water pot at the well and ran to tell other people in her city about this man who offered her life (verses 28–30). And those in her city believed. They believed the woman branded as an outcast. First because of her word (verse 39) and later because they experienced Jesus for themselves (verse 42).

God used the woman from Samaria to impact her entire community. He changed her character in one short conversation. She had a twofold impact—evangelistically and socially. She influenced her community socially because she became the impetus to bring together two diverse racial groups that had no connection whatsoever. It was so effective that Jesus went and spent the weekend with the Samaritans. She became the gateway through which Jesus came and stayed among the people in her community. Even though she was a woman with a checkered past, God used her to influence the lives of those around her, which goes to show that God can, and will, use anyone for His kingdom purposes when that person responds to His truth.[1]

How did Jesus refine the Samaritan woman's priorities? In your own words, explain the difference between knowing who Jesus is and knowing Jesus. How did starting a conversation with Jesus change the Samaritan woman?

Show Time!
Viewing and Examining the DVD Content

In this portion of the DVD, Chrystal Evans Hurst finishes the story about the Samaritan woman at the well from John 4.

After viewing the presentation "The Refining of a Kingdom Woman," use the following questions to help you think through what you saw and heard.

1. Read John 4:4–26.

"THE WOMAN AT THE WELL"

And he had to pass through Samaria. So he came to a town of Samaria called Sychar, near the field that Jacob had given to his son Joseph. Jacob's well was there; so Jesus, wearied as He was from his journey, was sitting beside the well. It was about the sixth hour.

A woman from Samaria came to draw water. Jesus said to her, "Give me a drink." (For his disciples had gone away into the city to buy food.) The Samaritan woman said to him, "How is it that you, a Jew, ask for a drink from me, a woman of Samaria?" (For Jews have no dealings with Samaritans.) Jesus answered her, "If you knew the gift of God, and who it is that is saying to you, 'Give me a drink,' you would have asked him, and he would have given you living water." The woman said to him, "Sir, you have nothing to draw water with, and the well is deep. Where do you get that living water? Are you greater than our father Jacob? He gave us the well and drank from it himself, as did his sons and his livestock." Jesus said to her, "Everyone who drinks of this water will be thirsty again, but whoever drinks of the water that I will give him will never be thirsty again. The water that I will give him will become in him a spring of water welling up to eternal life." The woman said to him, "Sir, give me this water, so that I will not be thirsty or have to come here to draw water."

Jesus said to her, "Go, call your husband, and come here." The woman answered him, "I have no husband." Jesus said to her, "You are right in saying, 'I have no husband'; for you have had five husbands, and the one you now have is not your husband. What you have said is true." The woman said to him, "Sir, I perceive that you are a prophet. Our fathers worshiped on this mountain, but you say that in Jerusalem is the place where people ought to worship." Jesus said to her, "Woman, believe me, the hour is coming when neither on this mountain nor in Jerusalem will you worship the Father. You worship what you do not know; we worship what we know, for salvation is from the Jews. But the hour is coming, and is now here, when the true worshipers will worship the Father in spirit and truth, for the Father is seeking such people to worship him. God is spirit, and those who worship him must worship in spirit and truth." The woman said to him, "I know that the Messiah is coming (he who is called Christ). When he comes, he will tell us all things." Jesus said to her, "I who speak to you am he."

Chrystal notes that Jesus spoke only seven statements to the Samaritan woman. In session 2, we examined Jesus' question and first statement, "Will you give me a drink?" Now let's look at Jesus' second surprising statement: "If you knew the gift of God and who it is that asks you for a drink, you would have asked him and he would have given you living water."

Notice that Jesus quickly turned the discussion toward deep and significant issues.

Is there a more important topic of discussion than knowing who Jesus is? What would you say to someone who asks you, "Who is Jesus?"

2. In Jesus' fourth statement, He challenges the woman to admit what her lifestyle is: "Go, call your husband and come back."

   The woman at the well answers, "I have no husband." And Jesus responds with a summary of her less-than-ideal matrimonial status. From that point on, the Samaritan woman is sold on Jesus' authenticity.

   Before the Samaritan woman could be changed, she had to be open and honest about her sinful lifestyle. Chrystal says, "We can't move past where we are because we won't be honest about where we're standing."

   Why must we admit our sins and shortcomings before God can use us? Why is it impossible to lie to God? Chrystal says that if you don't take responsibility for your sins, "you're only hurting yourself." What does she mean by this?

3. Read John 4:27–30; 39–42 (ESV), which is printed below.

"MANY SAMARITANS BELIEVE"

Just then his disciples came back. They marveled that he was talking with a woman, but no one said, "What do you seek?" or, "Why are you talking with her?" So the woman left her water jar and went away into town and said to the people, "Come, see a man who told me all that I ever did. Can this be the Christ?" They went out of the town and were coming to him. . . .

Many Samaritans from that town believed in him because of the woman's testimony, "He told me all that I ever did." So when the Samaritans came to him, they asked him to stay with them, and he stayed there two days. And many more believed because of his word. They said to the woman, "It is no longer because of what you said that we believe, for we have heard for ourselves, and we know that this is indeed the Savior of the world."

The Samaritan woman was feeling shame, guilt, and loneliness when she came to the well, but she left with boldness, bravery, and courage. It took only seven sentences for Jesus to transform her, to change her character and mind. He essentially said, "You can go and preach about me."

In your own words, tell why the Samaritan woman was willing to leave her pot and tell her community about Jesus. What changed her? Why does it take us so long to get excited about telling others about the Savior of the world? What would it take for you to leave your water pot?

4. Chrystal, quoting an unknown author, reads a list of several people in the Bible who had flaws. Take a few minutes to add to the following list, looking up these passages in a Bible: Job 1:21, Luke 10:40–42, and 1 Timothy 5:23.

Noah was a drunk.

Abraham was too old.

Isaac was a daydreamer.

Jacob was a liar.

Leah was ugly.

Joseph was abused.

Moses had a stuttering problem.

Samson had long hair and was a womanizer.

Rahab was a prostitute.

Jeremiah and Timothy—they were too young.

David had an affair and was a murderer.

Isaiah preached naked.

Jonah ran from God.

Peter denied Christ.

The disciples fell asleep while praying.

Zacchaeus was too small.

Paul was too religious.

Lazarus was dead.

None of God's messengers mentioned in the Bible were perfect, especially not by diamond standards. They all had obvious inclusions. Why is it important to do ministry or share your testimony even when you don't feel worthy? At what point does a woman become refined enough to share what she know about Jesus?

5. Read the following excerpt, and reflect on the questions at the end.

JESUS REDEEMS OUR FLAWS
by Chrystal Evans Hurst

While washing dishes after a family meal, I began contemplating the value of the pots and pans that I have. I remembered back to when I got married and received various pots and pans as wedding gifts. Each time I would cook, I would furiously wash them afterward to try to keep them looking new and unused. You can guess that my obsession with clean pots and pans didn't last too long, as more cooking blemishes appeared faster than I could clean them.

Growing up, I couldn't understand why my mother let her pots look "messy." Now, as a grown woman myself, I know why. Good cooks have seasoned pots and pans. My mother's favorite pans were usually the ugliest. My grandmother's all-purpose skillet was cast-iron—a veteran of many years. My Crock-Pot is priceless, but it has scuff marks of its own. If a pot or pan isn't marked up, then that would indicate that it hasn't been used.

We tend to look at people who have life wounds and wonder what has happened to them. Sometimes those battle scars are a result of struggles that person brought on herself. Sometimes that person may have had no fault at all in the acquisition of her injuries. From the outside looking in, we may stop and stare because we tend to dislike noticeable imperfections. The fact of the matter is that many women with scuff marks are simply seasoned and, therefore, more available for God's use because of their imperfection, inadequacy, or emptiness.[2]

Based on this excerpt, how can scuff marks on our lives make us even more valuable kingdom women? How can Jesus refine or redeem our imperfections and make us even better servants?

So What?
Helping It All Make Sense
The four Cs of a diamond are carat, cut, clarity, and color. There are many more Cs that describe a kingdom woman.

Take a few minutes to read through the "C Is for Christian" selection and do the activity at the end.

C Is for Christian

Christ can take your calamities and with the power of the cross, help them make your calling come to be.

If you cast your cares on Him, He will comfort you and He will carry you and He will give you His sense of peace and calm.

If you can stop being crooked and stop creeping and stop following the crowd and decide to crucify your flesh, then you will find that God can fill your cup to overflowing. He will be your mighty counselor. He will help you turn a corner. And He will confirm His will in your life.

And then you will find that you can rise up and be a kingdom woman.

But it doesn't stop there. You still have to continually confess your sins. He will make you clean. He will give you a clear conscience, and He will clothe you in a robe of righteousness.

And I'm not talking about something that I've read in a book. My name is Chrystal, and I stand before you because God had to have compassion on me. He did not condemn me when I was in my sin, but He has given me confidence to

stand here before you today. You are beautiful; you are valuable; you are a gem. You are a kingdom woman **c**reated in His
image.

And I pray that you will **c**ultivate a relationship with Him—
that you will be **c**onsumed with His Word. That you would
believe what He says about you and your situation. That you
would **c**omprehend with all the saints what is the depth of His
love for you. And that in Him you would find that with nothing
else, just Him, you are **c**omplete.

Take a few minutes to write down four Cs from this list that you
want to focus on this week. Write a personal prayer asking God to
show Himself to you personally and work on your character in these
four areas.

Transformation Moments
Taking the Next Step at Home
Read the following excerpt, and reflect on the questions at the end.

DROP YOUR WATER POT

by Chrystal Evans Hurst

A kingdom woman is the woman who is willing to abandon her own agenda, plans, and hang-ups to act on what God says. She, like the woman at the well, is willing to leave the water pot at the watering hole and take action.

My sister, the time is now. The people in your community need you now. The folks on your street need you now. The person who sits next to you at work needs you now. It's not about your perfection. God uses imperfect people. It's not about having your ducks in a row. God wants to help you line them up. It's not about being superspiritual or without sin. Jesus Christ has covered our transgressions with His blood and His sacrifice for you and me on the cross.

The time is now. There is no better time to respond to the call of God on your life than right now. You don't need to wait until your family is perfect or your salary is just right. Spiritual sainthood is not required. It matters not that your children are still little or that you have some weight to lose. Denominational divides are not a valid excuse for denying others God's love. Your upbringing is not a reason to avoid reaching out to touch someone else and share with her what you have received. The clock is ticking.

You are more than your past, the depth of your pain, or the number of your problems. You are who God says you are. You can do what God says you can do. You can have what He says you can have.

Be bold.

The longer you hold on to your water pot in fear of how you will maintain your anonymity or self-respect, the less time you have to share your life and your story with people who need to know Jesus can save. People are dying and need you to rush into the city to tell them about what God has done in the past and what He is doing for you right now.

The Samaritan woman didn't have it all together, but she met a man who did. Jesus offered her a way to get her life together by relying on Him.

God wants to use you. Yes, *you*. Your testimony, the same testimony that you avoid and try to hide, could be the very key to someone in your community seeing Christ—His goodness, mercy, and power.[3]

All kingdom women were encased in kimberlite before Jesus found them, mined them, and refined them. Kingdom women need to tell others how Jesus refined their lives. Don't wait. It's urgent.

4

THE HOPE OF A KINGDOM WOMAN

The Main Point

Jesus is the source of hope for a kingdom woman.

The Gathering

Getting Your Thoughts Together

To find out more about the source of all hope, read the following book excerpt and answer the questions that appear at the end.

HOPE IN THE PRINCE

by Tony Evans

There's a beautiful story about a beautiful lady. Her name was Cinderella. But Cinderella felt ugly. She lived with a wicked stepmother and two equally wicked stepsisters. They made Cinderella their slave. Now, she was beautiful, but she didn't think about herself as beautiful, because of the influence of a wicked environment that put her down, messed her over, and reduced her to nothing. The problem with Cinderella was that she was stuck there. She was locked in the situation, and for a long time she could not get out of it.

You've heard the story. You know about the ball and how she was miraculously transported there in a carriage. At that ball she met a prince. The prince saw Cinderella and loved her. But the problem in the story, as you know, is that the clock struck midnight, and she reverted to her old self. She became a slave again to an evil family.

The good part of Cinderella's story, though, is that the prince never forgot her. Even though a lot of people had been at the ball, something about Cinderella made her stand out from the crowd. She was special. She was unique. She was rare. Everyone wanted the prince, but the prince wanted Cinderella. All he had to work with to find her, though, was a shoe she had left behind.

If he could find the foot that fit the shoe, he would find Cinderella. So he set out going house to house in search of his treasure. After a long and hard search, the prince finally found her. Hope Incarnate knocked on her door.

If you feel trapped by your circumstances like Cinderella did, it's easy to lose heart. What I want to remind you is that there is hope. Jesus knows right where you are, and He knows how long you've been there. He has a way out of any hopelessness you may feel. He doesn't just want to bring His money to you, His castle to you, or His chariot to you.

He wants to bring you to Him. He wants to take you out of the bondage and let you live in the freedom of His presence and provision. He wants to show you your new position and your new glory. He wants to get you out of a spirit of slavery. He wants to give you hope.[1]

Do you believe there's a Prince? How would you describe your relationship with the Prince? Is He forever waiting for you to attend the ball and come to Him? Have you left Him standing at your door? Or have you selected Him as your first Husband and have confidence that eventually you'll live "happily ever after"?

Show Time!
Viewing and Examining the DVD Content
In this DVD segment, Tony Evans uses the history of the Susan B. Anthony dollar coin and the story *Cinderella* to explore themes of

hope in Jesus, aka the Prince of Peace. He also explores Luke 13, a story about a woman who needed healing.

⁓∞⁓

After viewing the presentation "The Hope of a Kingdom Woman," use the following questions to help you think through what you saw and heard.

1. Dr. Evans mentioned the Susan B. Anthony dollar, first coined in 1979. It was minted to honor a woman who was a leader in the women's rights movement in the nineteenth century. There was no women's rights leader in first-century Judea—except perhaps Jesus. Many women back then probably felt as if they were only quarters. The infirmed woman described in Luke 13:10–17 probably felt like a penny, if that.

   What is the one reason we know from the text that Jesus called out to this woman and healed her? Hint: It's in the list below.
   - Jesus had compassion for her.
   - The woman reminded Jesus of His cousin, Elizabeth.
   - Jesus wanted to show Satan a thing or two about His power.
   - She was a daughter of Abraham.

- She was a faithful synagogue attendee even though she had been suffering for eighteen years.

What was the one thing this woman had to do to be healed?

In what ways does this story inspire you to move toward Jesus?

2. Tony Evans says, "There is a difference between going to church and meeting Jesus at church. You can go to church and nothing happens, but you can meet Jesus and everything happens."

Do you agree with those maxims? Why or why not?

3. The bent woman is called the "crippled" or "infirmed" woman in some translations. On the outside, it appeared as if her affliction were physical. However, verse 11 says she had a spiritual affliction. Tony Evans says, "If all you see is what you see, you may not see all there is to be seen." What does Tony mean by this? Circle the correct answers—there are more than one.

- You may need glasses.
- You're looking only at the physical or external part of the world.
- There's another kingdom called the spiritual kingdom that can be seen only by discerning believers.
- Jesus could "see" into the woman's life and knew that her affliction was spiritual in nature and not a true physical limitation.

4. How can you know if you've made it past reading Jesus' résumé and have had the first interview? Which of these two scenarios best describes your knowledge of Jesus: (1) You have tasted from Jesus' spiritual menu, or (2) You are sitting at the table wondering what the price will be if you order?

If you would like more information about how to become a kingdom woman and accept the plan of salvation, you can find a YouTube clip of Tony Evans talking through the plan of salvation. It's called "Salvation Through Jesus Christ." The URL is http://www.youtube.com/watch?v=HSNayo631a0. Or you can pray the following simple salvation prayer that reinforces some of the concepts we've learned about Jesus so far in these sessions.

> "Dear Jesus, I confess that I am a sinner and my life is dirty. I believe that You are clean and holy and are seeking me because You love me and value me. I want to be found. I want You to remove my flaws. I want to move toward You. I now place all my confidence in You as my Savior. Please forgive me of my sins and grant me eternal life with You. Thank You for finding me and saving me. I want to live my life for You. Amen."

If you prayed this prayer, let your group leaders or pastors from your church know so they can rejoice with you and give you some material to help you learn more about salvation.

5. In the closing illustration, Tony Evans tells the story about a little girl in a grocery store with her mother. The girl sees the chocolate-chip cookies and badgers her mother for the treats. Her mother consistently says no. Then in the checkout line,

the little girl boldly prays out loud, beseeching God for the cookies. The other customers in line hear her and ask, "Why won't that woman buy her daughter some cookies?" The mother, embarrassed, breaks down and purchases the treats.

What was Tony trying to convey with that story?

6. Read the following excerpt, and reflect on the questions at the end.

 ## THE BENT-OVER WOMAN
by Tony Evans

Scripture has a story for us of a woman limited by bondage. She wasn't Cinderella, but she faced her own ongoing struggles that kept her from living out the truest form of her destiny. This woman who was unable to stand tall is in the book of Luke. It says, "A woman was there [in the synagogue] who had been crippled by a spirit for eighteen years. She was bent over and could not straighten up at all" (13:11).

Here we have a woman who for eighteen years had an unfixable problem that doubled her over. Like the hunchback of Notre Dame, she could not straighten up. Her eyes regularly saw only the ground because she was unable to look elsewhere. The passage makes it plain that there was nothing she or anyone else could do to straighten things up for her. She perhaps had some kind of spinal deformity that kept her bent over.

Because of her physical position, she could never fully see things as they really were. Her perception not only of herself but also of the world around her was distorted. Her issue was not just one of health, but it had become one of habit simply because it had gone on for so long. Eighteen years is a long time to have your world affected adversely by something you did nothing to deserve and have no power to change. This woman's life had to have been filled with discouragement day after day, week after week, month after month, year after year. It would be easy to assume that the woman may have lost her hope.

Are you able to identify with her—or with Cinderella—in any way?

Maybe you have experienced a pain or a problem that won't go away, and you feel stuck in a rut. Or stuck in a position that doesn't offer any hope for a brighter tomorrow. Before you give up on your problem, look up.

See, being a kingdom woman is about connecting with the One who gives hope. For a kingdom woman to experience spiritual victory or relief from whatever may keep her head or heart down, she has to go to Jesus.[2]

Based on this *Kingdom Woman* book excerpt, in what ways can you identify with the bent-over woman? With Cinderella? In what ways do you think the crippled woman's perspective changed after Jesus set her free? Has this story changed your perspective on God in any way? If so, how?

So What?
Helping It All Make Sense

Take a few minutes to read through the "Savior Who?" section and answer the questions in the self-test.

Savior Who?

The TV show *Doctor Who* is about a brilliant and eccentric do-gooder who travels through time with his companions. When normal Earth-dwellers first meet Doctor Who, he seems normal too. But by the end of each episode, Doctor Who's vast scientific and historical knowledge, unpredictable decisions, and advanced technologies expose him for what he is—an alien Time Lord who is hundreds if not thousands of years old.[3]

Like Doctor Who, Jesus probably seemed like a normal Earth-dweller at first glance. Nothing about His appearance attracted special attention (Isaiah 53:2). However, His words and His attitudes tipped people off that He was more than He seemed. And then there were the supernatural powers—those were a clear sign Jesus was different.

Take this short self-test to help you reflect on the actions of Jesus you've learned from the Luke 13 story of the bent woman and the John 4 story of the Samaritan woman. Do these reports show Him to be a Normal Joe or a Super Savior?

Indicate your answer by marking a spot on the line between "Normal Joe" and "Super Savior."

1. Jesus got thirsty after a long walk.

   Normal Joe   Super Savior

2. Jesus talked to the Samaritan woman, breaking down cultural barriers.

   Normal Joe   Super Savior

3. Jesus told her prophetic details of her life.

   Normal Joe   Super Savior

4. Jesus explained deep spiritual truths to her.

   Normal Joe   Super Savior

5. Many Samaritans believed that Jesus was the Christ.

_____

Normal Joe   Super Savior

6. Jesus preached in a synagogue.

_____

Normal Joe   Super Savior

7. Jesus felt compassion for a crippled woman.

_____

Normal Joe   Super Savior

8. Jesus healed the crippled woman.

_____

Normal Joe   Super Savior

9. Jesus explained deep spiritual truths to her and the synagogue rulers.

_____

Normal Joe   Super Savior

10. Jesus became popular because of His willingness to heal people.

_____

Normal Joe   Super Savior

Transformation Moments
Taking the Next Step at Home

Read the following *Kingdom Woman* excerpt, and reflect on the questions at the end.

FIVE HUNDRED DOLLARS

by Chrystal Evans Hurst

I needed five hundred dollars. After adding up all of my expenses and calculating the income I could bring in, I still needed five hundred dollars.

At the age of nineteen, I was a brand-new, unmarried, single mother in the middle of my sophomore year of college, and I was attempting to figure out how to make the numbers work so I could stay in school. I was vulnerable, at risk, and scared. Yup, that about sums up exactly how I felt.

I had done all I could do in terms of my own figuring. I'd looked for another job, cut expenses, and gone over the numbers more times than I could count. Exhausted in my own strength, I decided that my only option was to pray for a miracle.

Rights? Did I even have any rights? Did God's covenant extend to me in my situation? Could I call out to Him based on His Word and expect Him to answer me? I figured it couldn't hurt to try, so that's what I decided to try to do.

I cracked open my Bible and did what so many of us do when we need to hear a serious word from the Lord—I let the Book fall open and hoped that the word I needed to hear was on that page.

No such luck.

But I did start reading. I read on simply because I so badly wanted to hear from Him, and I was desperate to persist until I got what I needed. Eventually, I read right into the passage covering the story of David and Goliath, and I sensed that story was the one for me to stake my prayer request on.

Even after hearing that story over and over as child, I must have read it five times on this particular day. I was searching for the message in the story—my message from God. Honestly, the more I read it, the more confused I was! What was my giant? Was my giant to conquer staying in school and have faith in God's provision and His strength to finish? Or was the giant to trust God, yield to the change in my life, head home, and start fresh?

It was probably the middle of the night when I finally got up from the kitchen table and went to bed. I had read the passage over and over, prayed over and over, journaled my heart whispers on the matter—and still no clear answer.

Exhausted, I retired with empty hands.

It was only five hundred dollars. Many years later, I can look back on that one evening of my life and be amazed at how monstrous that five-hundred-dollar deficit seemed to me. If staying in college was my giant, then that dollar amount was my sword to slay it with. And I didn't have the weapon in my possession.

As the time grew closer for me to finalize my decision to return to school or stay in my hometown, I continued to ask God for the additional five hundred dollars needed to conquer the giant in front of me. I believed with my mind that the God who owned "the cattle on a thousand hills" (Psalm 50:10) could find a way to sell a couple of those cattle on my behalf. I had rehearsed many times my belief that "my God will meet all your needs according to his glorious riches in Christ Jesus" (Philippians 4:19). So like Gideon laying out his fleece, I laid out my desires before the Lord and waited for Him to answer definitively.

He answered. At the last minute, the mail arrived with a letter addressed to me from someone I'd never met. I opened the letter and out fell a check for five hundred dollars.

No kidding. For real. Exactly five hundred dollars.

And true to form, God's blessing didn't stop there. He continued to bless me "exceeding abundantly above all that we ask or think" (Ephesians 3:20, KJV). In fact, this initial monetary gift was the first gift of many that God would send me through a precious family throughout my time in college until I graduated.[4]

Chrystal didn't feel like a powerful kingdom woman when she was nineteen. She didn't feel as if she had a special "right" to claim God's favor. The only thing going for her was her commitment to reading the Scriptures and a stubborn hope that God would take care of her. So she prayed persistently, and God lovingly provided.

Ask yourself these questions: What need do you have this week that Jesus can meet? How persistent will you be in turning toward Jesus, asking Him to meet that need? How can you become available to meet the needs of someone else?

5

THE LEGACY OF A KINGDOM WOMAN

The Main Point
Faithful kingdom women can leave a positive legacy in their home, church, and community.

The Gathering
Getting Your Thoughts Together
To find out more about living well so that you have a positive legacy to leave, read the following book excerpt and answer the questions that appear at the end.

 ### THE LEGACY OF A SINGLE WOMAN
by Chrystal Evans Hurst

I remember my aunt and the example she has always lived in excellence—that's her legacy to me. Never married, she dedicated herself solely to the Lord and has given herself to be "Auntie" to her nieces and nephews and now her great-nieces and great-nephews in so many ways. She also dedicated herself to starting and running the children's program at our church for decades— while simultaneously getting her PhD. She is a woman of excellence, and when asked what motivates her to be that way, she will reply, "Because of that day."

"That day" is her reference to the day that she expects to stand before Jesus and the day He will test the quality of her work. The truth is that we all will face "that day," and if the service we have offered Him is excellent, we will hear those blessed words, "Well done, good and faithful servant. . . . Enter into the joy of your master" (Matthew 25:23, ESV).

Like my aunt, I want to hear those words. I want what I do and what I have done to make Jesus smile on that day. A life of excellence isn't easy. There aren't always accolades, especially when you choose to make important the things that are important to the Lord. But there will be one very meaningful accolade on "that day."

Excellent is what we will be when we are made perfect in the next life. However, in the meantime, our job is to strive for the excellence the Father has revealed to us in the season of life that we are in, in the context of our lives right now. And as we commit to pursue this life, the life of an excellent woman, the Father transforms us into the likeness of His Son.

Psalm 16:11 says, "You have made known to me the path of life; you will fill me with joy in your presence, with eternal pleasures at your right hand." Choosing excellence now is to choose the fruit of joy and pleasure in days to come.

When we choose excellence, God gets the glory.

When we choose excellence, we benefit from walking in the fullness of His joy on earth and investing in the pleasures of eternity in heaven. When we seek excellence, we leave a legacy for our children and for others in the community.

So, my friend, choose the excellent way. And do so not for the reasons that you can see but for the things which are not seen and that are eternal (2 Corinthians 4:18).[1]

You are an example to others—you have no choice about that. But you do have a choice about what kind of example you'll be. Chrystal's aunt chose to live an excellent life, and that example is part of Chrystal's spiritual legacy.

What people in your life are most likely watching you? Would they say you are living an excellent life? Why or why not? Who gets the glory when you choose to be an excellent example? Explain your answer.

Show Time!

Viewing and Examining the DVD Content

In this DVD segment, Lois Evans shares the legacy stories of her maternal grandmother (called Granny) and her mother. Those two women both "knew Somebody."

After viewing the presentation "The Legacy of a Kingdom Woman," use the following questions to help you think through what you saw and heard.

1. Both Ivy and Annie (Lois's grandmother and mother, respectively) made do with little money. Ivy even had to move into government housing after her husband died. But neither of these women complained. In fact, they had great joy. Consider the following verses and select the one you think best describes Lois's legacy:

    - Philippians 2:14, "Do everything without complaining or arguing."
    - 1 Timothy 6:6, "Godliness with contentment is great gain."
    - Hebrews 13:5, "Keep your lives free from the love of money and be content with what you have, for God has said, 'Never will I leave you; never will I forsake you.'"

2. God changed Lois's mother's plans of being a missionary to being the mother of eight children. Do you think that, in reality, she fulfilled both callings? Why or why not?

3. Lois refers to "Somebody" throughout her talk. She calls that Somebody the King of Kings and Lord of Lords. Lois also refers to being a daughter of the King, of royal heritage. How does knowing "Somebody" affect how you live your life? Do your kids, other family members, coworkers, classmates, fellow church congregants, or roommates know that you know Somebody? What kind of verbal feedback do you get? Do people mention that you walk as if you "know Somebody"? What's the difference between being confident in the Somebody and plain old pride?

4. Lois says the promise of God's blessing is available to those who choose to obey God. Do you agree with this statement? Why or why not? What's the difference between being humble in our sinful state, knowing that God needs to clean us up and refine us, and the obedience that He desires so that He can bless us through a generational legacy (see Deuteronomy 28:1–9)?

5. Read the following excerpt, and reflect on the questions at the end.

THE LEGACY OF "TWO MAMA"
by Chrystal Evans Hurst

As I write this reflection, I am so very blessed to still have both of my grandmothers alive and available to speak into my life on a regular basis. My maternal grandmother, "Grandma," will be ninety-four soon, and she is planning to embark on yet another cruise in a few weeks. My paternal grandmother, "Two Mama," calls me without fail if she feels like I've gone too long without calling her. If she doesn't call, she sends me an e-mail in ALL CAPS, clearly conveying her disapproval of my lack of communication.

Yes. At almost eighty years of age, my grandmother sends e-mails to me. Both of my grandmothers are alive and kicking.

But since time waits for no one, I'm conscious that the time I have with each of them is precious and that every phone call, every visit, and every kiss on a well-worn cheek is a priceless gift.

The funny thing about watching grandparents or parents age is that I see the people in my life who have always been the strongest, the most in-charge, and the most together slowly morphing before my eyes. They move from a state of perceived independence into a season of dependence.

Recently, my lovely Two Mama has had some health challenges. After years of being a diabetic and having multiple surgeries to maintain good blood flow to her extremities, Two Mama had to have one of her legs amputated. She had gone to the hospital in so much pain. And she's a strong woman, so if she said she was hurting, it must have been really bad. Over the next couple of days, her doctor determined that nothing else could be done to save the leg.

I wasn't there. I couldn't hold her hand. So I did the next best thing and called many times a day. On one of those phone calls, I could hear her crying out in anguish.

The pain was just too much, and I heard my strong grandmother expressing that guttural sound that only true agony knows. My dad, who was in the room with her at the time, put the phone to her ear and told me to talk. "Two Mama, I love you. I'm sorry you are in so much pain. We all love you and are praying that all will be well soon. It's gonna be okay. You are gonna be okay."

In between her waves of throbbing trauma, I heard her say, "God is good, baby. I have to trust Him. God is good."

Where does someone get that kind of faith? Where does a woman find the strength to speak well of her God in the middle of intense pain, hurt, distress, discomfort, or difficulty?

I still consider myself to be in the middle of my own faith walk and don't have the strong fortress of faith my grandmothers have both attained in the face of a lifetime's exposure to good and not-so-good times. However, I know this to be true: The kind of faith my grandmother showed that day and in the days ahead is the kind of faith that can only be built brick by brick and day by day as a woman walks committed to God's purposes and plans for her life.[2]

Write down some memories of kingdom women who have invested in your life.

So What?

Helping It All Make Sense

Take a few minutes to read through the "Write Your Own Obituary" exercise, and answer the questions that follow it.

Write Your Own Obituary

Alfred B. Nobel changed his life after reading an obituary—his own. When Alfred's brother Ludvig died in 1888, the newspapers printed an obituary of Alfred in error. The obituary truthfully described Alfred as the inventor of dynamite, a substance that not only made Nobel very rich but also made it possible to efficiently kill more people than ever before. Mr. Nobel was horrified that he would leave a legacy on improving mass murder. Shortly afterward, he used his great fortune (roughly comparable to 250 million dollars in today's economy) to institute the five Nobel Prizes, among them the Nobel Peace Prize.[3]

Take a few minutes to write your own obituary, or if that's

---

too grim, write a letter to a child or close friend explaining what type of person you are today.

Now write a description of the kingdom woman you'd like to become; be detailed about the legacy you desire to leave.

Keep this page handy to reflect upon when you pray or read your devotions. Keeping these goals in mind is what Lois would call "living on purpose," part of the legacy her mother left to her.

Transformation Moments

Taking the Next Step at Home

Read the following excerpt, and reflect on the questions at the end.

THE LEGACY OF ROSA PARKS

by Tony Evans

The year was 1955; the location Montgomery, Alabama. The environment reeked of racial toxicity predominantly manifested in the segregation of the Jim Crow South. Although mere inches separated row eleven from the whites-only seating area on the bus driven by James F. Blake, it represented an abyss that existed between the equality and justice experienced by white and black citizens at that time.

Sitting in row eleven was a quiet, introverted, yet determinedly strong woman named Rosa Parks. A white man boarded the bus, and the driver—a man who had previously taken Rosa's money and driven off before she could board the back entrance of the bus—sought to demean her one more time.

Rosa recognized his face as he turned to tell her to get up and move so that the white man could sit down. Who could forget those eyes, steel-like and unfeeling? Rosa had just attended a course on social and economic injustice earlier in the year, a course in which nonviolent protests had been emphasized. Yet as a lead investigator assigned to sexual-assault cases against black women by white men for the previous decade, including the infamous gang rape of Recy Taylor, Rosa knew full well what noncompliance could ultimately lead to. She had every right to seek self-preservation and move.

Even so, Rosa would later remark that the memory of the brutally slain young black boy Emmett Till at the hands of white men played prevalently in her mind when James F. Blake told her to move. And because of that, she couldn't do it—no matter what risk she took. So Rosa Parks remained seated in row eleven.

They say that actions speak louder than words, and you can tell what someone truly believes by what he or she does. Rosa's lips never offered an explanation to the white man standing with an air of entitlement beside her, waiting to sit down. Yet the forty-two-year-old woman's actions spoke with such great volume that an entire nation couldn't help but hear.[4]

Her simple yet profound decision to refuse to give up her seat to a white man who had demanded it, to no longer accept the indignity of second-class citizenship, and instead to proclaim both her value and rights as a child of God altered the trajectory of America forever. This one act led to the birthing and maturing of the Civil Rights Movement as we know it, improving the lives of countless individuals simply because Rosa decided to both maintain and retain her dignity.

Rosa will forever be remembered as the mother of the Freedom Movement. Her children are legion, her influence acute, and her legacy significant.[5]

Only God knows how far the legacy of a kingdom woman will spread. Consider any relationship or responsibility you have as a legacy—it's your choice whether the legacy is positive or negative.

What are some decisions you need to make this week in order to make sure your legacy is a strong one? If you don't have children, are there some younger people whom you can influence? For those of you who work outside the home, how can you impact your work environment this week? For those of you who are timid, how can you build your faith so that you can be bold for the kingdom?

THE POTENTIAL OF A KINGDOM WOMAN

The Main Point

The impact or potential a kingdom woman can have is unlimited.

The Gathering

Getting Your Thoughts Together

To find out more about the potential of a kingdom woman, read the following book excerpt and answer the questions that appear at the end.

KINGDOM WOMEN WHO
REALIZED THEIR POTENTIAL

by Chrystal Evans Hurst

God's Word is full of stories of women who walked the path of faith and realized their potential. Those women found out that it is worthwhile to trust that God is who He says He is and that He will do what He says He can do.

Like Rahab, believe God to set you free from a lifestyle that does not please Him.

Like Hannah, believe that God hears the guttural longings of your soul.

Like Ruth, believe that God can carry you through devastation and loss so you can dance again.

Like Bathsheba, believe that God's goodness can supersede the consequences of a bad decision.

Like the woman at the well, believe that God can satisfy your deepest thirst.

Like Mary, the woman with the expensive perfume, believe that to offer Jesus the best of everything you are and everything you have is never a worthless pursuit.

Like Mary, the mother of Jesus, believe that God can use regular gals like you and me to deliver great things to the rest of the world or to the mission field within our own homes.

Your potential is the same because that same God is your God: "Know therefore that the Lord your God is God; he is the faithful God, keeping his covenant of love to a thousand generations of those who love him and keep his commands" (Deuteronomy 7:9).[1]

Do you believe that God can use "regular" kingdom women to deliver great things to their homes? How about to "the rest of the world"? If not, why not? How far do you think the potential of just the kingdom women you know can reach?

Show Time!
Viewing and Examining the DVD Content

In this DVD segment, Chrystal Evans Hurst tells the stories of three biblical Marys: Mary, the mother of Jesus; Mary of Bethany; and Mary Magdalene.

After viewing the presentation "The Potential of a Kingdom Woman," use the following questions to help you think through what you saw and heard.

1. On a scale of 1 to 10 (with 1 being "I would have done just as Mary did" to 10 being "I would have run away to the circus to escape this job, angel or no angel"), how eager would you have been as a teen to find out you were pregnant by the Holy

Spirit? How do you imagine your family would have reacted? What would you if you had a daughter and she came home with this news? Who are the Elizabeths in your life—the people you can turn to when you need spiritual support?

2. Mary didn't ask the angel a lot of questions. Her meekness included a total trust that God would take care of the details. God seems to provide information to His followers on a need-to-know basis. How can "needing to know" too much slow us down when God asks us to be unquestioningly obedient?

3. Chrystal quotes Ann Voskamp, author of *One Thousand Gifts*: "To lack faith isn't as much an intellectual disbelief in the existence of God as fear and distrust that there is a *good* God."[2] The three Marys could have doubted God's goodness: Who would ask a good Jewish girl to be an unwed mother? How

could a beloved brother's death be good? How could dying on the cross at the hands of the Romans be anything but evil?

If a kingdom woman doubts God's goodness, what is a likely result?

4. One lesson we learn from Mary of Bethany is that time spent with God is never wasted. A second lesson is this: God treasures our extravagant worship. Why don't we, like Mary of Bethany, desperately crave time with Jesus, sparing no expense to worship Him and learn from Him? What can you do to open your heart so that He's your first love?

5. Mary Magdalene "ministered" to Jesus and the disciples before His death. Afterward, she was the first to see Jesus after His resurrection, and she began the work of spreading the news that He had risen. Chrystal asserts that the ministry in one season of your life may lead to ministry in the next season. What ministry are you doing today? What ministry would you like to be

doing in the future? How do you see God preparing you for a ministry in the future? If you don't have a ministry now, what small contribution can you make toward helping the church or one of its members?

6. Read the following book excerpt and answer the questions that appear at the end.

DISTRACTIONS
by Tony Evans

When we allow our priorities to fall into disarray, we can count on some pruning. God will not stand by and watch something else suck the life out of a potentially fruitful branch. One of the interesting things about distractions is that they can be good things in and of themselves. Distractions aren't always negative things that take us away from what is good. Frequently, they are good things that take us away from what is better. The biblical story of Martha and Mary emphasizes this point clearly.

While Jesus was traveling from city to city sharing the good news, He entered a certain village where two ladies, Martha and Mary, lived. Now, even though Jesus was with His disciples—and everyone knows that if you invite thirteen preachers into your home, it means you are going to have to prepare a rather large meal—Martha took it upon herself to welcome Him and His team for dinner.

However, in the midst of preparing this enormous meal, an issue came up between the two sisters. Apparently, Mary had started out helping in the kitchen but had found her way to Jesus' feet, captivated by what He was saying. We know all of this occurred based on what Martha said to Jesus: "But Martha was distracted by all the preparations that had to be made. She came to [Jesus] and asked, 'Lord, don't you care that my sister has left me to do the work by myself? Tell her to help me!'" (Luke 10:40).

Jesus' reply to Martha gives us one of the most significant insights into our relationship with God. He said, "Martha, Martha . . . you are worried and upset about many things, but only one thing is needed. Mary has chosen what is better, and it will not be taken away from her" (verses 41–42).

In His statement, Jesus affirmed that Mary had chosen the better thing. The things that had distracted Martha were not bad things. In fact, they were good things that she was doing for Jesus. However, the very things Martha was doing for Jesus distracted her from Jesus.

Martha hadn't been disobeying God in her meal preparations, but she had become so involved in them that she excluded herself from time with Christ. Essentially, her calendar had become filled with cooking rather than being with her Savior. Often when women come to me for counseling because they are struggling in their lives, it is not because of ongoing sin. Nor is it because they are bad people. Most of the time, the issues have developed because of the overabundance of good things that they are trying to accomplish simultaneously, thus leading to their priorities being out of kilter.[3]

What does the phrase "the good is often the greatest enemy of the best" mean? What are some good things in your life that may distract you from the best things?

We all have a little Martha in us. We all have responsibilities, and certainly Jesus wasn't suggesting that Martha and Mary never clean their home. How do you know when you're supposed to be serving and when you're supposed to be sitting at the feet of Jesus?

So What?
Helping It All Make Sense
Take a few minutes to read through the "Mary Makeover" self-test and answer the questions that follow it.

Mary Makeover

Indicate your answer by marking a spot on the line between "Not Like Mary" and "Just Like Mary."

1. To submit to God, I would be willing to have my reputation ruined and my life plans changed at the drop of a hat.

   Not Like Mary   Just Like Mary

2. To submit to God, I would believe an angel who foretold a great miracle that would upset my life dramatically without asking a single question.

   Not Like Mary   Just Like Mary

3. To submit to God, I would praise Him for the honor of having my life changed to serve Him.

   Not Like Mary   Just Like Mary

4. To focus on God, I would unhesitatingly allow guests into my messy house and serve them crackers and cheese sticks so that I could spend more time reading my Bible.

   Not Like Mary   Just Like Mary

5. To focus on God, I would not worry about displeasing my nagging sister. I would take her criticism with a smile—if I could just spend a few more minutes listening to a Tony Evans sermon podcast.

_____

Not Like Mary   Just Like Mary

6. To focus on God, I would take all my available savings (three quarters of my annual salary before taxes) and donate it to a missions organization that feeds the poor.

_____

Not Like Mary   Just Like Mary

7. To minister to others, I would happily follow around a group of ragtag men who are wandering the countryside sharing the gospel. Oh, and I would pay for their lodging and food, too.

_____

Not Like Mary   Just Like Mary

8. To minister to others, I would swallow my grief, pain, and shock at having just seen a man gruesomely executed, and I would help anoint his battered body and prepare it for burial.

_____

Not Like Mary   Just Like Mary

9. To minister to others, I would risk looking the fool and telling others I had seen a dead man's fully resurrected body.

_____

Not Like Mary   Just Like Mary

How did this exercise help you identify areas that you need to grow in? What's one thing you can do this week to focus more on God, be meek and submissive, or worship in an extravagant manner?

Transformation Moments

Taking the Next Step at Home

Read the following excerpt, and reflect on the questions at the end.

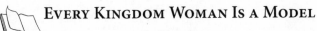

EVERY KINGDOM WOMAN IS A MODEL

by Tony Evans

On a trip to New York City with my wife, I visited Macy's. Just outside the store were windows lined with mannequins to lure passers-by to come in. On this particular day, we noticed that a number of individuals had gathered outside one of the windows. So we decided to walk down and check it out. In the window stood several well-dressed mannequins. Yet when we looked closer, it appeared that these mannequins were blinking their eyes.

As we stared at them, we soon realized that these were real models posing as mannequins in an attempt to direct people's attention to the kingdom they represented—Macy's.

As the people gathering outside the window began to detect that these were live models, they started to wave their hands and make odd faces in an attempt to get the models to break their poses. Grown adults did all sorts of contortions trying to distract the mannequin models. Yet the models held firm, accomplished their purpose, and piqued the interest of numbers of people who eventually went inside, lured by the attraction. The models were able to hold firm to their purpose because they weren't distracted by the commotion. Their job was to impact the world that was passing by rather than be impacted by it.

As a kingdom woman, you represent a King from another kingdom who has put you here on earth as a preview for all that He offers and can supply.

Your job is to impact your family, church, community, and world, which are passing by, rather than be impacted by them.

A number of voices seek to distract you, and many of those voices are even good, but God has given you a purpose to represent Him and His kingdom on earth.[4]

As with the Samaritan woman, that will require boldness. As with Mary the mother of Jesus, that will require submission. As with Mary of Bethany, that will require focus. As with Mary Magdalene, that will require a willingness to serve. Yet as with all of them, the fruit will bear a legacy resulting from the power of God's grace and worthy of Christ's name. What are the marks of a kingdom woman who is reaching her potential? In what area of faith would you like to improve this week: boldness, focus, risk, or _____? What is one practical step you can take this week to come closer to being a fully formed kingdom woman?

Notes

Session 1: The Value of a Kingdom Woman

1. Adapted from Tony Evans and Chrystal Evans Hurst, *Kingdom Woman* (Carol Stream, IL: Tyndale, 2013), 9–11.

2. *Strong's Concordance*, s.v. Hebrew 5828 *ezer*, http://biblesuite.com /hebrew/5828.htm and s.v. Hebrew 5048 *neged,* http://biblesuite .com/hebrew/5048.htm.

3. Eleanor Roosevelt, as quoted in *Reader's Digest*, September 1940, 37:84.

4. Adapted from Evans and Hurst, *Kingdom Woman*, 13–14.

5. Adapted from Evans and Hurst, *Kingdom Woman*, 18–19.

Session 2: The Making of a Kingdom Woman

1. Adapted from Evans and Hurst, *Kingdom Woman*, 191.

2. Most Expensive Diamond, "Top 10 Most Expensive Diamonds in the World," accessed September 21, 2013, http://mostexpensive diamond.org/ and Dina Silverberg, "The 5 Priciest Diamonds in the World," *Diamond Envy: Rare Thoughts* (blog), September 12, 2012, http://www.diamondenvy.com/blog/the-5-priciest-diamonds -in-the-world/.

3. Gemological Institute of America, "Diamond Clarity Grades," accessed September 22, 2013, http://www.jewelry1.com/diamond /DIACLARI.htm.

4. Adapted from Evans and Hurst, *Kingdom Woman*, 192.

5. Barry Gutwein, "The History of the World Famous Cullinan Diamond," *DiamondVues* (blog), March 31, 2005, http://www .diamondvues.com/2005/03/the_history_of.html.

6. Adapted from Evans and Hurst, *Kingdom Woman*, 77–80.

Session 3: The Refining of a Kingdom Woman

1. Adapted from Evans and Hurst, *Kingdom Woman*, 190–191.

2. Adapted from Evans and Hurst, *Kingdom Woman*, 63–64.

3. Adapted from Evans and Hurst, *Kingdom Woman*, 192.

Session 4: The Hope of a Kingdom Woman

1. Adapted from Evans and Hurst, *Kingdom Woman*, 31–32.

2. Adapted from Evans and Hurst, *Kingdom Woman*, 32–34.

3. Doctor Who TV, "Who Mysteries: The Doctor's Real Age," October 19, 2012, http://www.doctorwhotv.co.uk/who-mysteries-the-doctors -real-age-37396.htm.

4. Adapted from Evans and Hurst, *Kingdom Woman*, 123–124.

Session 5: The Legacy of a Kingdom Woman

1. Adapted from Evans and Hurst, *Kingdom Woman*, 53–54.

2. Adapted from Evans and Hurst, *Kingdom Woman*, 81–82.

3. Bio.True Story, "Alfred Nobel," © 2013 by A&E Networks, accessed

September 30, 2013, http://www.biography.com/people/alfred-nobel
-9424195.

4. Jennifer Rosenberg, "Rosa Parks Refuses to Give Up Her Bus Seat,"
accessed April 25, 2013, http://history1900s.about.com/od/1950s
/qt/RosaParks.htm; Facing History and Ourselves, "A Pivotal
Moment in the Civil Rights Movement: The Murder of Emmett
Till," http://www.facinghistory.org/resources/units/pivotal-moment
-civil-rights-moveme; Christopher Klein, "10 Things You May Not
Know About Rosa Parks," History.com, February 4, 2013, http://
www.history.com/news/10-things-you-may-not-know-about
-rosa-parks; and "The Montgomery Bus Boycott: December 5,
1955–December 26, 1956," accessed April 30, 2013, http://web
cache.googleusercontent.com/search?q=cache:UIdWWXUT3bo
J:www3.pittsfield.net/groups/parkerchandler/wiki/welcome
/attachments/135be/Bus%2520Boycott%2520Begins.

5. Adapted from Evans and Hurst, *Kingdom Woman*, 197–198.

Session 6: The Potential of a Kingdom Woman

1.   Adapted from Evans and Hurst, *Kingdom Woman,* 84–85.

2. Ann Voskamp, *One Thousand Gifts: A Dare to Live Fully Right
Where You Are* (Grand Rapids, MI: Zondervan, 2010), 148.

3. Adapted from Evans and Hurst, *Kingdom Woman,* 138–139.

4. Adapted from Evans and Hurst, *Kingdom Woman,* 196–197.

About Our Presenters

DR. TONY EVANS is the founder and president of The Urban Alternative, a national ministry dedicated to restoring hope and transforming lives through the proclamation and application of God's Word. For over three decades, Dr. Evans has also served as senior pastor of Oak Cliff Bible Fellowship in Dallas. He is a prolific author, including the best-selling *Kingdom Man* and *Kingdom Woman*. His radio program, *The Alternative with Dr. Tony Evans*, is heard daily on more than 850 radio outlets. Dr. Evans is also the chaplain for the Dallas Mavericks and former chaplain for the Dallas Cowboys. He is married to Lois, his wife and ministry partner of over forty years. They are the proud parents of four: Chrystal, Priscilla, Anthony Jr., and Jonathan. For more information, visit TonyEvans.org.

CHRYSTAL EVANS HURST is a gifted writer, speaker, and worship leader. She is the eldest child of Dr. Tony and Lois Evans, so the Word of God has surrounded and guided her for her entire life. As a member of Oak Cliff Bible Fellowship, Chrystal assists her mom, Lois, in leading the women's ministry and loves to encourage women toward a deeper relationship with the Lord. Her blog—*Chrystal's Chronicles*—poignantly reflects her thoughts about her faith and day-to-day experiences. Most important, Chrystal is a dedicated wife and homeschooling mother of five.

LOIS EVANS, author of the insightful *Seasons of a Woman's Life*, has been employed by the Billy Graham Evangelistic Association, the Grand Old Gospel Fellowship Ministry, as well as numerous executive management positions with The Urban Alternative since its inception in 1982. Lois is also founder of Pastors' Wives Ministry.

She serves in the office of the Senior Pastor at Oak Cliff Bible Fellowship Church, National Religious Broadcasters Board, and The Urban Alternative Board of Directors. She recently received The Woman of the Year in Ministry Award presented by the Women of Influence, Inc.

However, her most impressive credentials are that she "knows Somebody," and she is a daughter of the King of Kings.

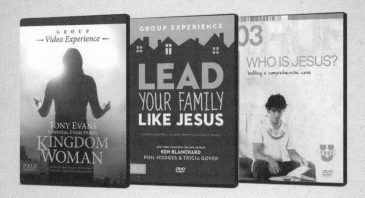

Kingdom Woman Book and *Kingdom Woman Group Video Experience* $10 Rebate

GET A $10 REBATE

when you purchase both the *Kingdom Woman Group Video Experience* and *Kingdom Woman* hardcover book. Both titles must be purchased at a retail store to qualify. Simply return the completed rebate form (original or photocopy), the original dated store receipt(s) for both products, and the UPC bar code from both packages (original or photocopy) to: Kingdom Woman Rebate, Attn. Customer Service, 351 Executive Dr., Carol Stream, IL 60188.

(978-1-58997-743-3)

(978-1-62405-209-5)

NAME _____

ADDRESS _____

CITY _____ STATE _____ ZIP _____

E-MAIL ADDRESS _____

STORE WHERE PURCHASED _____

SIGNATURE _____

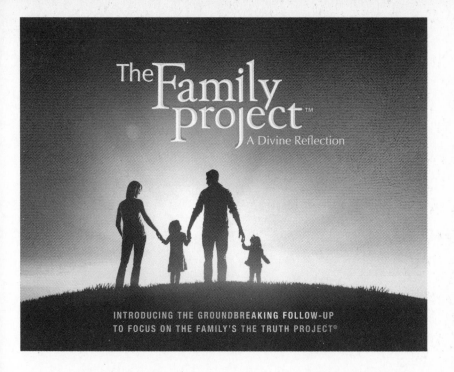

The**Family**
project™

A Divine Reflection

INTRODUCING THE GROUNDBREAKING FOLLOW-UP
TO FOCUS ON THE FAMILY'S THE TRUTH PROJECT®

THE PROFOUND IMPACT OF BIBLICAL FAMILIES

From the creators of the life-changing series *Focus on the Family's The Truth
Project®* comes a stunning new journey of discovery that explores family as a
revelation of God—and the extraordinary impact families have on the world
around them. Introducing *The Family Project*™, a transformative, feature-
length documentary and DVD curriculum that reveals—
through an in-depth exploration of God's design
and purpose—biblical truths about the role of
families in society.

VISIT
FamilyProject.com
TO LEARN MORE

FOCUS ON THE FAMILY®

Welcome to the Family

Whether you purchased this book, borrowed it, or received it as a gift, thanks for reading it! This is just one of many insightful, biblically based resources that Focus on the Family produces for people in all stages of life.

Focus is a global Christian ministry dedicated to helping families thrive as they celebrate and cultivate God's design for marriage and experience the adventure of parenthood. Our outreach exists to support individuals and families in the joys and challenges they face, and to equip and empower them to be the best they can be.

Through our many media outlets, we offer help and hope, promote moral values and share the life-changing message of Jesus Christ with people around the world.

Focus on the Family MAGAZINES

These faith-building, character-developing publications address the interests, issues, concerns, and challenges faced by every member of your family from preschool through the senior years.

THRIVING FAMILY® Marriage & Parenting	FOCUS ON THE FAMILY CLUBHOUSE JR.® Ages 4 to 8	FOCUS ON THE FAMILY CLUBHOUSE® Ages 8 to 12	FOCUS ON THE FAMILY CITIZEN® U.S. news issues

For More INFORMATION

 ONLINE:
Log on to
FocusOnTheFamily.com
In Canada, log on to
FocusOnTheFamily.ca

 PHONE:
Call toll-free:
**800-A-FAMILY
(232-6459)**
In Canada, call toll-free:
800-661-9800

Rev. 3/11

More expert resources
for marriage and parenting . . .

Do you want to be a better parent? Enjoy a stronger marriage? Focus on the Family's collection of inspiring, practical resources can help your family grow closer and stronger than ever before. Whichever format you might need—video, audio, book or e-book, we have something for you. Visit our online Family Store and discover how we can help your family thrive at **FocusOnTheFamily.com/resources**.